Author of

- *The Sex Allegory and Other Poems* (Poetry)
- *Bonas Divas* (Novel)

FEMININE TESTAMENT

Louisa Lum

Miraclaire Publishing
Kansas City (MO)

MIRACLAIRE PUBLISHING LLC
Kansas City, (MO) USA

Email: info@miraclairepublishing.com
Website: www.miraclairepublishing.com

ISBN-13: 978-0615709611
ISBN-10: 0615709613

Copyright © 2013 Miraclaire Publishing LLC
Priscillia M. Manjoh

All rights reserved.
No part of this publication may be reproduced by any means, graphic, electronic, or mechanical, including photocopying, recording, taping or by any information storage retrieval system without the prior written permission of the copyright holders.

Printed in the United States of America

Miraclaire Publishing makes every effort to ensure the accuracy of all the information ("Content") in its publications. However, Miraclaire and its agents and licensors make no representations or warranties whatsoever as to the accuracy, completeness, or suitability for any purpose of the Content and disclaim all such representations and warranties, whether expressed or implied to the maximum extent permitted by law. Any views expressed in this publication are the views of the author and are not necessarily the views of Miraclaire.

What is on a woman's mind is a woman,
We gossip, and we trash,
We hate and love each other.
It's our prerogative

Society Girl

I
She turns heads everywhere
She goes; men's frowns
Metamorphose when their glance meet hers.
She is poised and collected;
She knows
She owns the world,
SOCIETY GIRL
Checking out all opportunities
To get ahead, and the world
Bow to her;
They want to
do her.
SOCIETY GIRL,
Nothing to stop her
No one to stand in her way
SOCIETY GIRL,
pretty as a picture
Sagacious as the queen of Sheba

II
All sticks and stones, negative
Comments don't touch her
As long as she gets what she wants.
Husbands!
Husbands!
The infernal chant of
Un-ambitious women.
Who roof houses with the lot?
Men are in droves and the higher
A woman climbs the social ladder
The better her pick.
No woman
Can own one of these beasts,
THEY
Are untamed terriers always
Forgetting their way home -
Home is home.

III
Making money is what
Really matters, how much
You make is what you can
Control, no emotional *wahala*[*]
After work is normally pleasure!
All work without play makes
Jennifer a geek.
You go through the lot and
Pick one -
They are all
The same under the sack.
You just need to show
You are an experienced
Canine trainer.

---

[*] Pidgin English word for "problems"

IV
All sticks and stones
That negative talk about
Unmarried women.
Husbands!
Husbands!
No one has ever thatched
A hut with green hay.
Global warming won't
End just because all women
Have got themselves
HUSBANDS.

V
All sticks and stones
That bashful criticism
That comes not from
My incompetence in the
Job I do or my lousy
People skills but from
The fact that I am unmarried
Does it make me a society girl?
Must I go crying about:
'Husband!
Husbands!'
No one roofs a house
With the kind.
The Massacre in Syria
Won't stop because
All women had such
A one. The hungry of
The world won't get
Fed because all women
Were conveniently married.

VI

All sticks and stones
All water on a duck's back
All empty steam
To all those who have
Nothing better to do with
Their time they dedicate
to lip service,
Society girls never cry
'Husbands!
Husbands!'
No one thatches
A hut with the type,
the misery in the World is still there
though I have one:
HUSBAND

Has Been

I
When I was in Calabar,
Men used to worship me like
A goddess.
I had a temple and
A band of faithful spellbound
Fools.
I was young then,
Pretty too,
The world was mine
To conquer.
I could cause a bigger
Trojan war with a flick of my little
Finger, I was that solicited.

II
When I was in Dakar, in the
Good old days when people
Still valued women with an
Education, I was the toast
Of the university, beauty
With brains. Femme fatale
All the freshmen
Followed me around like lap dogs
I only had to say a word and it was
Law. I was a deity and everyone
Accorded me my rightful dues
I was young and stunning,
Beauty that brought tears to
The eyes and gave men
Weak knees. That was when
I met Douif, we were young
And I was searching for adventure.

III
When I was in Paris
I was the joy of Montparnasse
The cafes were glittery and the
Patrons knew me personally.
They paid me to patronize
Their businesses.
I particularly adored M.
Andre, he was such a *cheri*
And his *fine au base de cognac*
Was heavenly.
I enjoyed the haute cuisine
At M. Flaubert's, the steak
Au source the champagne
Was DE-LI-cious.
Paris! That Bohemian
City of epicurean bliss.
That was where I encountered
My Jean Paul, he was refined with
The soul of an artist, I married him
Though we are not together anymore

IV
When I was in Hong Kong
I was happy in the crowd
The orients have experiments
You can't ever dream of
They have subtle ways
Of eliciting pleasure
Karmsutra was written
In India but it was totally
Edited in Hong Kong,
I have a tattoo to remember
The times when I was a
Society girl.
That was when I fell for Sing Ling
He was the most charming man
In the world, with delicate features
And bags of money. It was fun discovering
The world in his prestigious yacht.
We married on that floating mansion
Though we are not together anymore.

V

When I was young, I was
The trend setter,
The muse of great poetic
Ejaculation of the young
And the foolish,
I was always the belle
Of the place.
When I was young, the poet's
Corner came to being,
Every author was inspired
By me. When I was young
Men worshiped at my altar
They still do.

House Wife

I
Leave my husband alone
Cheap prostitute, husband snatcher
He has responsibilities at home
Stop trying to lure him to the world
He picked me over all of you loose
Women, you wasted your opportunities
And now that your bloom of youth is fading
You try to destroy my marriage
Leave him alone, shameless harlot.
Ashawo[+]!

II
Leave my man alone you daughter of Jezebel
Stop giving him rendezvous to sleazy motels
Let him be, Madam Prostitute, I will not allow
You to tempt him into evil ways
A married man has no business with a single
Woman, don't send him text messages
Don't greet him if you pass him on the street
He is my husband and my duty is to protect
Him from the wails of painted ladies like you

[+] Prostitute

III
Look how she seats on my own settee
Waiting for me to wait on her
She has no right to be here
Shameless woman! Husband thief!
I know his wife, I will surely report
This travesty, how dare she show her face
Where decent women tread? She clings on
The arm of another woman's man
And simper like a hussy, I spit in her
Drink as I will spit on her grave when
My friend has her head for trying to
Covet what is another's.
Bitch! Husband snatcher
That I should entertain her

IV
Ugly handmaid, no man wants you.
You try to harvest where you never
Sowed! You think you have the nerve
To filch what is mine, just so you know
He's out for adventure, we laugh at you
Every night, at your pathetic attempts
To tie him down, you are such a fool
If you so think that you can put asunder
What God diligently set together.
I am the house wife, you, the fucking
Bitch. Men are buccaneers who will
Take from willful despicable women,
Women of no repute.

V
Married women are talking,
This is serious talk, let single girls
Stay quiet, this are family matters
What do women who have never
Walked down the aisle know about
Such talk?
Stop gibbering, house wives
Are planning, this is serious talk!
Marital issues.
What do you have to contribute?
Women who have never seen the color
Of a marriage certificate.
Stop chattering! Old handmaids!
What do you know about
The care and attention of a husband.
You'll never get up
      with a blissful smile on your face.
Quit yapping, this is serious talk.
Married women talk.
You have nothing to add,
When have you
Been introduced
      as the spouse of a proud man?

Wanna be

I
Single and Seriously Searching
There she sits, looking chic
Groomed as a Barbie
Sampling vintage as a pro
Perched as though on top
Of the world.
Waiting to get picked
Waiting to be proposed marriage

II
I wanna be married, I need
A man to take care of me
Married women have a great time
Of it, they have no problems
They have nothing to bother their
Pretty heads but to be pretty
I wanna be married, it is my
Soul's most fervent wish

III
I wanna be married, to a rich
Handsome man, we will attend
Parties every day, and I will have
Different dresses for different occasions
Sundress for breakfast, cocktail dress for
Lunch and the robe noir for dinner,
Every married woman sleeps in peace
They don't worry
their pretty heads about breakfast.

IV
I wanna be married, to an adoring
Husband, with seven kids and a puppy
We will have a house in the suburbs
And neighbors will gossip about us
Junior will be an engineer just like
His daddy, Annie will be a poet
Jenny will be beautiful just like
Her Mama and Mark will be strong.

V

I wanna be married, I am very ready
Single and seriously searching, I will
Be married, armed with a marriage brochure
The stage is already set, all we need is the
Final peg to fit in the square hole, a handsome
Rich and adoring husband.
I wanna be married and married I will be
I have laid all the ground work and traps.

Angry Spinster

I
I am an angry spinster
Angry at the world
I refuse to conform to what you
Think I should be, I refuse to sit
And pine, yearning for what could be
I will not live on false expectation
I try to live life, I try to celebrate
My singleness. But society constantly
Finds fault and dub me a spinster.

II
I am a spinster, angry at the world
I refuse to be slammed down
By the weight of disappointment
That crops up from the numerous heartbreaks
I refuse to waste from desperation
I refuse to succumb to the pain
Of rejection,
As others are constantly picked over me
I refuse to submit to the trauma
Of lies and fake promises
I refuse to regret that I am the marginalized single
In a world of valorized pairs.

III
I am an angry spinster, angry at
A fickle world, that has no sympathy
For those who cannot conform.
I am an angry spinster
But
I am no Havisham, not me
I won't build a hall of fame
For fellows who come to slice
Away pieces of my heart
I won't construct a monument of hate
For miscreants who have attempted
To sap my confidence and leave me uncertain.
I won't write hate letters and dedicate curses
To men who only wanted to tick me on their
Lists of conquests.
No!
I won't, because I need my time and energy
For the quest of things I can control
I won't, because I need time and energy
To molding my soul and improving my mind

IV
I am an angry spinster, angry at friends
Who blame me because I am single
Who say being single is an illness
And that I brought it on to myself.
My friend, if I make a closet of all
The wedding dresses that I never wore
We will need a warehouse to showcase all
If I write a book of all the fairy tales
That were too fragile to survive
Then we will have encyclopedias.
My friend, you say it's all my fault,
That I have an attitude problem
That I am too enthusiastic about life
That I don't know how to pretend
That I can't keep my feelings to myself
That I don't dress like a born again
That I am too independent
You see my friend, you can't
Change the spots of a leopard
Every human being has a right
To be here, I am just asserting mine.

V
I am an angry spinster, angry at men
Who want me to dampen my expectations
In an attempt to flatter their little egos.
Men who try to subvert my
Capacity because I am a woman
Angry at the liver hearted ones
Who can't stand my excess enthusiasm

VI
I have been a cheerleader, supportive
Enabling him to win many a challenge
But he still ran off,
I have been the confidant, listening
And giving advice,
He too fled.
I have been sassy, bringing
Happiness
Yet he disappeared
I have gone on my knees
And asked the good Lord
To give me what he deems
Mine, I won't belabor the point.
What is mine will find me,
I am blessed enough.

VII
I am an angry spinster!
I am disgusted at a short sighed world
One that judges me without knowing me
Confidence is a gift that comes with probity
Yet mine is taken for arrogance
I am an intelligent woman, I love heated debates
Men who can't compete say I talk too much
I am a beautiful African woman, with curves
I love to celebrate. My suffrage mothers fought
That I be liberated. I don't go naked,
If I am too hot for, poor you
I won't apologize for it.

VIII
I am an angry spinster
But!
No more pining
No more crying
No more yearning
No more searching
What's mine, if it was mine will find me.

IX
I am an angry spinster
Yet!
No more sack clothing
No more sweat
No more bother
No more sighing
What's mine, if it was mine will surely find me.

X
And to you my friend,
I celebrate you, though like me
You are a wanton human being
All I ask is a return of the favor
But if you can't thanks, no qualms
If singleness is a disease, I might find
The antidote! It just might not be labeled
MAN.

Anxious Mother

I
Children these days are
Filled with the modern shit
They think they know better
Than their poor mothers,
They claim they are independent
Love living single, having careers
Guzzling alcohol and partying till
The wee hours of the morning.

II
What a real woman needs is a husband
Alhadji was often cruel and cold
But he was my husband, put a roof on
My head and catered to my needs too
What a good woman needs is a husband
It lends her respectability.
With a husband your life has meaning
You have a job -to make him happy

III
Mariama my first is such a shrew
She is filled with this tasteless
Feminist shit that modern women
Have convinced themselves is en vogue
She talks too loud, drinks a man under the table
And dresses like a lady of the night.
Poor Alhadji! He will have a heart attack
If he was alive, may his soul rest in peace
In our day, a good woman wore the purdah
A man would have been very lucky to see an ankle.

IV
Allah be praised that my Fatimatou
Is such a sensible one, she is firmly
Married and has given me seven little
Ones. Her kids and husband occupy her
And she is not idle. An idle woman is
A feminist devil's workshop.
A woman can only be gainfully employed
If she is taking care of a man. A woman's
Husband is her king, even though he might
Only have one eye.

V
Jamilatou is as bad as Mariama
She is blatant and has pierced
And tattooed her body like a
Porcupine. She laughs at me
When I complain, she says I am
Old fashion. She is a business
Woman and though she is doing
Well I still disapprove. The business
World is no place for a woman,
If a woman has time to have
A job other than her husband
And children, it should to be
A teacher like my Fatimatou.
A business woman
Is as bad as a male nurse.
I still worry, where did I go wrong
At least Fatimatou is proof that I tried.

Happy Widow

I
Dear husband, I consider
You as such though you were
Nothing but a cheap ass bastard
This is my eulogy, now that you are
Death I am completely free of your domination
You were a man of great wealth yet
I wallowed in poverty, went about in rags
I was patient and now that you are deceased
I am finally getting my reward.
I am taking your Prado for my personal car.
I just tasted wine and I will be having
A bottle of the finest every night with dinner
I have been shopping and you need
To see my makeover.

II
Rest in peace treasured companion,
this is my eulogy
You were a whoring spouse who cared nothing
About the sentiments of his wife,
Those are all bygones, you are death now
And there is no reason to hold a grudge
Against the death.
But I will be taking a trip to the Caribbean
It is a pleasure trip if you are wondering
I am travelling first class all the way and back
I have made reservations in a five star lodge
I hear they have a first class spa
With handsome eunuchs willing
To please a paying customer's every whim

III
Darling demised spouse, this is my
Epithet to you, I know it will be
Tacky to dance on your grave, but
I am doing the best I could to improvise.
You use to kick and slap me around
Because I was your mobile punching bag
There is no reason to bear scruples
Against a ghost. Nice has always been
Wasted on you.
Now that you are death, I made
A garage sale of your expensive
Designer dresses, I could have given
Them away but I wanted to make sure
To do something you'll disapprove of.

IV
Beloved husband, this is my tribute
To you, it was very kind of you
To die as you did. The sickness
Was quick to claim you so we didn't
Deplete our resources on ineffective
Remedies. You were inconsiderate
In life but did me one appropriate
good turn by not clinging to existence
like the leech that you really are.
Now that you are death
I am touching up my hair color and
Lightening up my complexion too
I will be hanging out a lot with the
Girls and really catching fun too

V
Dearly departed husband, this is my last
Word to you. All the businesses you
Favored over me are still striving, but as
It is I need the time to enjoy the proceeds.
So I am selling them off and giving half
The proceeds to charity. You should
Be weeping in the underworld because
You have never given a dime to the needy.
I will make a good name out of your sweat
Goodwill ambassador, Madam Philanthropist
I do not look forward to meeting you in the
Other world, our contract is breached and your
Ghost cannot haunt me.

The Other Woman

I
Hello my love, I apologize
I am so far away, but you know
Daddy is got to work, kiss your
Little brother for me, please hand
The phone to mama, you know my
Sweet, your man is got to make a name
I wish you were there with me all along,
Though I am far,far away I think of you
By the second, nothing I do will mean
A thing if I don't feel your support.
The other woman must be silent, she can't
Move a bone for fear the wife will hear on
The other side, she is drained of all emotion
And though she loves him too,
It is evident it doesn't mean a thing.

II
Hello honey, you know you are the love
Of my life. You were with me when I was
A nobody, you believed in me and I know
I am the best because of your certainty.
I know that fame is carrying me the world over
The bad thing with celebrity is
that you are so solicited.
All I want is to be in your arms, right now
Nothing else matters,
She cowers in the shower like a thief
She too loves him as much and does
Everything for him to be more successful
If he had noticed her, she will be on the other
End of the line. But as it is, she knows he's so
Convinced that she is just a gold digger.

III
Allo ma cheri,
Did you arrive in one piece?
How is the Alps at the moment?
Do you
Remember our honeymoon,
We both
Learned to skate
Had such a good time
We were freshly in love
And learned to
Support and empower each other,
You are the best and
I know none can compete with you.
She adores him too,
And would have given
Anything to make him her hero, she cringes
Under the sheets because she didn't know
Him then, and now though he is a man and
Must have his pleasure, he doesn't care whether
She lives or die.

IV
My wife is so terrific, a real bombshell
Beauty with brains and my kids are all
Little geniuses.
You need to see the tricks
Little Johnny can pull and he is only nine
Little Angie can count up to twelve and
She is only three.
Awesome right?
She is cold as a statute, the dinner
Has lost all taste and it was really
Delicious.
She wishes someone would
Talk about her in that tone.
She will love
To have terrific kids too,
but her good intentions
Always gets flush in the toilet.

V

I am home my beloved, come over
And give daddy a kiss,
I have conquered
The world and will harvest the stars for you
I had so many challenges,
I could not surpass
Them all but I know
you'll forgive me.
She on the wrong side of marital bed
Cherishes him as well.
His skillful lies
Are still very effective,
her heart beats
In tandem with the clock though he
Will never come back.

Gold Digger

I
I have seen it all,
There is nothing
Love is over rated, what counts
Is the cash,
The posh cars and
Expensive clothes
Who has not seen love,
Who has not
Labored for that lie?
I loved him as much but
He broke my heart,
All I want now is to
Live and led live.
Give me money and I will
Be yours, give me gifts
And I will adore you.
Buy me a car
And you can ride me too.

II
Do you have money?
I know you
Love me,
But everybody claims
To love me as well,
You know I am
A beautiful woman and every
Gorgeous dame needs maintenance
If you have preserved money and
Courage to compete in the senior league
As your elders, then I might be yours.

III
I know you might love me more
Than God loved his beloved son
I know you might cherish me more
Than the Cameroon policeman
Cherishes a five hundred franc note

I know you might value me more
Than the price of gold on the world market
But that is all hot breeze in the air
That is all talk without action
All a lady needs is care,
Cash is the exchange

IV
I acknowledge you may admire me
More than Yeats did Maude Gonne
I agree you could esteem me
More than Romeo did Juliet
I affirm you possibly will respect me
More than Macbeth did his lady,
But I know the wiles of men
I am immune to all their ambushes
Because conquest is all they yearn for.
Give me money, and I will lay down
My life for you. Give me plenty money and
I will be yours as long as it keeps coming.

V
Tell it to the stars that you are
In love with the lady of the meadows
Shout it to the mountains that you are
Ensnared with the wench of the vale
Holler to the birds that you are
Enamored with the bird lover
That my friend is hot vapor
With no momentum,
I loved and he
Was false, all I need is your gold.
Hard cold gold to keep me warm
When the world is false. Shiny
Gold to buy me bubbles of happiness.

VI

Preach it to the unconverted that
You are the love of my life
Sermonize it to the heathens that
You are the soul converter of my soul
Lecture it to the birds that
You made me what I am
All I care for is what you have in
Your poach, all that matters is the miles
That you can go to reach my goal.
All that is important is the comfort
That your wealth can bring.
Quit the talk and let's to action
Make a financial statement, money speaks.

VII
I am a gold digger and I am proud
I dig diamonds too, pearls are quaint
Rubies are red, emeralds are green
Turquoises are gold and that is my favorite
Color too. I am a gold digger I have an
Eye for a fake, I sight posers a mile off
You know who I am and you come willing
I hold no weapon to your head.
You give cheerfully like the biblical giver
God loves you too.

The cheating bitch

I
I am a two timing bitch
I married you but Junior
Might not be your child
I am a scheming wench
And I forced you to proposed
Cos I had a lot at stake
You know the baby is not yours
I know you are wondering what
Is real but you weren't ever in the picture

II
Burn the bitch!
Drive a stake into her heart
Splash holy water on her face
Sink lumps of garlic down her throat
Shove a ring onto her finger!
I laugh at your feeble attempts
Burn a bitch, roast a bitch, stake a bitch
Marry a bitch, a bitch will always be a bitch.

III
I am the royalty of cheats
Your friends aren't safe
From me, I will grab at them
Even under the dining table
I am the crowned champion of
Cheating lovers, I shall go
Down in history as the BITCH!
Everyone should be good at something

IV
I am a no good cheat and you know it
You love hate me but you stick around
You are a brute for punishment it seems
I love the look on your face
When you catch me red handed
Giving the mail man head
I adore the anguish in voice
When I answer the phone with a moan
I know you know that I am up to no good.

V
I am a cheat it rhymes with cheap
It is a real tasking job, you have
To keep it up or people might get
The wrong idea that you are retired
Or cured. Give false impressions
Never let your guard down, make
Belief you are in the club though
You are only in the church. I am
Cheat, it's a credible title to hold.

The Unfulfilled woman

I
There he lies with a cocky grin
As though he has conquered the world
Is it too much to ask, just to have it once?
But how can it be,
when he concentrates solely
On his pleasure,
he jumps on me,
grunts like a pig
No matter how hard I try,
No matter what I do,
I get nothing
Lord, give me an orgasm,
Is that too much to ask?
That fairy tale about sexual bliss is overrated.

II
Give me an orgasm
that is my simple request
Stop covering up
with insincere gifts
Give me fulfillment,
it shouldn't be that difficult
You kept bragging
about your prowess in bed
Give me ecstasy
that is what I signed up for
I keep hoping and you fail to deliver
Give me pleasure
that is what you promised
Don't plead amnesty,
there will be no appeal.

III
Give me an orgasm,
 that is my humble plea
Kisses and roses,
stars and angels
That should be the outcome
when wooed
By one you love.
Stars and angels will
Come
to earth when there is love
They will descend
when lovers tangle
Poor me,
only pencils and rulers
Dreary me,
only displeasure
and sleeplessness.

IV
Provide me with an orgasm,
that is only a request
This museum will look
LESS BLEAK
if you could
Only grant me that little favor.
This stale familiarity
WILL LIGHTEN
if only you could lend
that desired return
These cuffs will look
A LITTLE LESS RUSTY,
if once in a while
You stand up to the bargain
These placid kids will look a little
HANDSOMER
If you could stand up to the occasion

V
Gift wrap an orgasm
for me this Christmas
It eludes me all the time,
I hear it is better
To fake it,
fake or real I never get any
You dance the ancient ballet,
making moans
And groans
but comes out empty handed.
I get the tail end of the barter–
UNPLANNED BABIES!
Please, man of my life,
This Christmas
Gift me with an orgasm,
you can dress like Santa.

Heartbreakers

When these pundits
Sycophants of woman's
Emotions come to us
In sheep's clothing
Extrapolating pontifical
Sermons of Forever after
Our poor hearts cannot emanate
A chill glacial enough to brush
Them off.
We succumb under
This charm and become simpering
Conquests.
And like every subdued
Entity we forget nothing good ever comes
From an invasion.
The disaster comes
Soon enough for
After the bittersweet passion,
HEARTBREAK!

Mixed Signals

They all want me
None of them can stand me
They run when I scream
They flee when I am mellow
They scuttle away when I act nice
They dash out when I am sassy
They constantly send mix signals
Love/hate, they want me, they can't stand me.

He loves me/ he loves me not

He loves me,
He loves me not
When he won't look into my eyes
When he averts his gaze
When he feigns being busy
When talk becomes a drag
When he feels loving me is betraying another
He loves me not.

He loves me not,
He loves me
When his stare follows me across the room
When he brushes my hand as if by accident
When he laughs at my bland jokes
When we hold hands and muse over nothing
When he needs me to share a private thought
He loves me

He loves me
He loves me not

Before you were mine

Before you were mine,
Mike came along, a shape changer
And a chameleon, butter won't melt
In his mouth, he was a dashing charger
He could never tell a lie, confidence
Incarnate, earnest as hell, reliable as weather.

Before you were mine,
There was John, a tormented dreamer
With a writer's soul,
he needed a muse
And tryst with me on the journey called life.
I was his joy and also his damnation
In his eyes I was:
The femme fatale in Keats' ballads
The Maud Gone in Yeats' laments
The Phlora in Angira's satires,
Sam was a poet,
A man after my own heart
I was a good muse,
but all muses inspire
Just the same, he had to move on
One muse is as good as the next.

Before you were mine,
There was Andy,
he was such a dandy

With the enormous ego
of all handsome dudes
He craved attention
but had none to give
He could be romantic,
when he wasn't preoccupied
With himself.
He knew the act of gift giving
What he couldn't give emotionally
His purse compensated.
He knew the best restaurants and
the best Vintage that France,
Australia and California
Had produced. He had a taste of life and
Shared once in a while.

Before you were mine,
There were a lot others, their faces
Have blurred, I remember nothing
Much about their characters,
but I still have some
Expensive gifts.
Life is a long walk and
Most times a lady gets a lift even when
She doesn't ask for one.

www.ingramcontent.com/pod-product-compliance
Lightning Source LLC
Chambersburg PA
CBHW050114170426
43198CB00014B/2579